Also by Jared Smith

This Town
co-authored with Kyle Laws
(Liquid Light Press, CO, 2017)

To The Dark Angels
(New York Quarterly Books, NY, 2015)

The Collected Poems of Jared Smith: 1971-2011
(New York Quarterly Books, NY, 2012)

Grassroots
(Wind Publications, KY, 2010)

Looking Into The Machinery: Selected Longer Poems by Jared Smith
(Tamarack Editions, PA, 2010)

The Graves Grow Bigger Between Generations
(Higganum Hill Books, CT, 2008)

Where Images Become Imbued With Time
(Puddin'head Press, IL, 2007)

Lake Michigan And Other Poems
(Puddin'head Press, IL, 2005)

Walking The Perimeters of The Plate Glass Window Factory
(Birch Brook Press, NY, 2001)

Keeping The Outlaw Alive
(Erie Street Press, IL, 1988)

Dark Wing
(Charred Norton Press, NY, 1984)

Song Of The Blood: An Epic
(The Smith/Horizon Press, NY, 1983)

SHADOWS WITHIN THE ROARING FORK

SHADOWS WITHIN THE ROARING FORK

NEW POEMS
BY JARED SMITH

FLOWSTONE PRESS

First Flowstone Press Edition, November 2017
ISBN-13 978-1-945824-15-9

**Dedicated to my Wife,
Deborah Parriott Smith**

CONTENTS

I

II

III

SHADOWS WITHIN THE ROARING FORK

I

Deep In The Convenience Store

A man buys two pens
   and puts them in his pocket
in the convenience store
the cash register accounts for two pens
   as two wide angle cameras take him in
side the cameras four more pens
click into the man's pockets
and the bar code reader sends data
while the parking lot camera scans two pens
clipped onto a sweat stained shirt, and
by the time he gets home 18 pens
bulge in his pocket, closing him in
while computers trace two pens back
to an assembly line in eastern Asia
where caps are placed on these things.

The man lies awake all night. His pens become immense and
do not have enough ink to write poems of the people he has touched.
His pens have meant more to people than all the poems he writes.
He knows his pens are filled with hungry haunted nightmares.

How Do You Look At This Space?

Growing old I write colder in fire,
more to lose and therefore words are gold
en fleece, are the sacred ark of the covenant,
the vessel of the blood which is eternal life,
the mythology of which insanity is formed,
the vessel which is the craft that poets study,
abandoning it in the years when flesh is young
and dying before reconciling themselves to
becoming the deserts that surround them. You
have not read many poems like this in academia.

I open fewer visions into the meanings than I
used to when sitting in bar rooms with high strung girls
because no seduction is needed, no love will save me
except any part of my soul that will escape the flesh,
and I have little hope of that since science is science.
I look instead to solid things that have had meaning.

I look to the structures we have surrounded ourselves
with, to the hallowed weathered boards we have formed
our structures with, the stores, the homes, the factories,
the dreams still undefined which we have lost in time,
our families, our children, our schoolyard memories,
the space that we have encircled in time to call ours.

I give it a key, and I hold it out to you, to open what.

One could say it is a box in time,
a cubicle spanning the space of stars
as the world goes on its uncharted way,
and there are many ways to get inside
but for a certain fee you get a metal key
opening doors to your child's future,
to the desks where college applications
will go whistling across the country and

dropping down on institutional blotters,
or maybe where you will be sitting when
the cancer that gets you comes calling,
but what is important is what's in it now
because the seeds of everything are here,

so you put the key into its lock and there are
books on shelves that lead back into the room
and maybe there are words on the pages you
haven't read yet or perhaps you have forgotten
and it might be this is the foyer of your frame house
and it might be that this is more of a used book shop
located between a diner at the corner of Main
and a Great Clips barber shop, a hardware store
on the other side, a coffee shop or odds and ends
that change from year to year as owners fade,
but each word remembers its author's voice
and page on page each book chants its harmony
and thank goodness the books go back and back,

because when you look at the key as it lies
on the front desk near the cash register, and
you pull back it becomes a part of the town
where you live in a vast uncomprehending maze
that matches the mountains and valleys complexity
as you pull back farther on your Google maps
and the building you own the key for disappears,
and once again, how do you look at this space?
I could go on and on but only with your presence.

There Be Monsters Where This Goes

I

All maps are drawn as much to obscure
the lairs of monsters dozing at their centers,
whether painting Main Street's route to the Bank
or the subways running from Wall Street to Town Hall
they limn the edifices important to their authors.
And though we believe them they are flat
in a round world deeper than Dante's *Inferno*
and omit the hardships that lie along their lines,
any one of which could erase the goal of going.

It is a Hellish way to go
within those pencil thin lines.
What of the naiads and nymphs
flittering within moonlit nights
that other men have never seen?
What of the one who takes you
from the home you were born to
to the faces you will meet lost
in the folds of what is known?

II

I don't know where this goes on the map,
what little lines or abstract symbols give it its worth.
I don't know how asteroids impacting on planets
change its meaning, though I suspect not much.
I don't know how the flow of money and politics
will effect your flesh or progeny, but I do know this:
These are the lines that are not set by the fates,
but are the ones that you find scuffing your feet
barefoot in the alleys behind the houses where you grew
where the streetlamps were shattered by the homeless
and the broken glass shattered their shadows at dawn.

I know that these are the maps that matter now
when you have gone so far from what you learned.

III

Driving a city highway you are the long thin neural network
running the spinal column of the body electric,
each streetlamp a vertebrae
                    each office light a node
each apartment in each high rise condominium
            an input expanding around itself
that you gather into your awareness.
At its core, love is a gazillion bar stools
in ten quadrillion states of mind in the cloud
            forward
backward across time held static
                    hyperlinked perplexity real time.

A car moves toward a tiny town of 200 souls
in western Colorado at 10 p.m.
and the driver is a compound of mountains
with a handful of kitchens, wood burning stoves for heat
he is aware of the Earth and not the grid,
of the network of rivers into lakes and time.

A plane passes over the country
each light below it human consciousness
dreams in a very distant night that breathes.
You think that you are flying the plane
            just as every other passenger
in all this vastness you follow the lines
and you are on the grid.

IV

Somebody has thought the whole thing out—
the reason for being/what happens in death/what goes on,
but has no formal education and no words to explain
and knows there's no reason to say anyway.
Just keeps you wondering. Words are like that
printed on billboards or scratched into the earth,
shocked onto digital tapes or hollowed into the wind.
A woman with dark hair, perfume, and blue eyes
lives down an alley between the folds of a map.
She has been waiting from before she was born,
buys sheets at Target and gowns at Saks and sings
to a melody you have never known never will.
The artists come and go as she grows old.
Bankers' eyes glitter through pin box telescopes.

V

And so, your flesh is softer than I can imagine
and your will is the only force I have encountered that scares me
and I am lost somewhere between those two,
and the maps were drawn long before we started out
but it is peaceful sitting here in the void with you.

The Devil's Window is a Binary Screen

It   is

•

a   spot
smaller than the universe
carry it with you

O

It is the digital screen you watch romantic comedies on
        lovers made of celluloid
the black notebook you carry your lover's photos in
        stripped of flesh and scent
the network nodes of your professional life in dots and zeros
the place you sit with your evening drink to watch wars and murders
        committed noncommittally in your living room
narrated by smiling faces on the evening news and commercials

•

So transparent and yet so translucent with resonance of life
it can be folded over put in your pocket used to call the stars
for positioning in the universe or to the bars in the darkest alley
or for naked selfies sent out to blackmailers and secret services
and its depth is endless and its messages are forever and are seen
by every server who serves us now and in the future.

O

And we pay for it a lot because it draws us in
the light within its darkness like moths to flame
thinking its numbers and images are anything.
        (and they are—anything at all)

We pay for it with our salaries and our minds
and we pay for it with the hours it absorbs
                    so little and so much
while the eternal darkness is still creeping up on us
and everything on it is kept everywhere else
and the universe itself is a big big place.

·

It is used for the naked and the dead and dying
for the personal and impersonal shadows of our lives
indistinct of meaning but sharp between its pixels
all on that one commercial lens of light and dark
with homeless men shambling toward tomorrow
and heroes doing things that no one does but heroes
and the cans of beer in the refrigerator growing cold
and the moths battering against the glass of night
and the trees rattling their dead branches in the wind.
It is a small, small thing of shattered desire
in so many sizes now that we can carry it anywhere
and the message is always one dollars falling useless
in a window that brings light from dark and dark from
                    zeros

O

The City Within The City

is within the darkest brick alleyways
at the far end, over the cobblestones
behind the greyest most modest wall
where when the doors open chandeliers
(cut glass from the hard hands of Tiffany)
shaken by Brahms and Mozart notes,
where shadowed men speak in whispers
slurring their words in aged whiskey or
rolling their vowels in brandy snifters
come together in every city nameless.

It is a place where Roman Cardinals
take off their shoes, turn water into wine
and pass bread among poor fishermen,
a place where Rothschilds sew buttons
onto the very fabric of industrial society,
knowing what seam clothes the factories,
what clothes the university professors,
and where the owners of the deepest mines
crush the land itself into the finest jewels.

It is a place linked by placelessness,
stretching across one continent to another
identified most by the silence of *gravitas*,
the number of communication lines run in,
the generations that have grown in-bred
that own the media that no one writes of,
that is the heartbeat that fills our lives.

Found almost always where least expected
it wears the dappled camouflage of soldiers
who have enlisted on the wings of angels,
and its music, its heady perfumes, baubles,
metaphysical incantations, whispered siren songs
are the darkest deepest richest fabric woven
in the city within the city within our home.

Nestled in The Foothills

I start this work as other men have done at my age
by digging down among the roots and what feeds them.
I have torn my hands already on lesser things, lost blood
and worn my flesh away for more than half a century,
chased thoughts on spots of ink in worn out books,
seen stars in the night from which we all have come,
have eaten the tubers grown thick on rich black loam,
and still somehow have not touched the ribosome
that turns in time all this reflective matter of the sun
into our flesh, our office buildings, subway stations,
living rooms and elusive data sets of similes. All talk
and talk of thought and thought itself is similes.

What does it matter now,
the coins in coffee cups,
the dollars and checks in coffers
cigarettes spit out in rain-soaked alleys
the stain of your lips on tobacco spikes
the stain of your lips on words gone
the grease from roadside diners
their red neon lit up.
Today again the ghost dance
shambles on heavy feet across my cabin
seeking new light from the shadows.

My healthy friends grown complacent are dead.
And the woman I once would have died for is dead.
Her perfume follows me in taxi cabs, silent nights,
shadows that obscure whatever follows me. That's
all right, she used to say. It is all right. I know
it is all right, but that it needs something from me,
something that hides beneath my shirt and beats drums
though I no longer carry coins in my pockets for Cerberus.
I hear a rustling behind the morning coffee cups,
and I know damn well it is not *The New York Times*.

Perhaps it is a stray thought caught in marmalade
and the brightness hidden within it is the song of cardinals
red feathered and black hooded against the white of winter,
holding berries in their beaks red as the spawn of wild trout in streams
that rise from the earth beneath dark, vast boulders hidden but alive
with all the dark bleeding misery and joy of what becomes us,
trying to raise awareness that even after all these years so little is said
in the words that men choose to read when there is time to be.

He Does What It Takes

Curling his fingers around porcelain
he cradles the morning cup of coffee and watches
steam rise between his fingers, how each finger
shapes the fog of morning with his unique mark,
his DNA and his fingerprints upon the swirl of time,
and he listens to the tick of the clock upon his wall,
the first birds beginning to sing in his garden,
and a dog startled by dawn down the street,
the morning paper hitting with a thud at his door.

This is what the man is before he goes out
to turn the ignition in his family car. It is what
his wife thought of before she thought of diamonds
and before there were other souls beneath this roof.
It is the little things that make the man what he is,
the scent of his chemical balances, the colors he sees
as sun rises over the blasted buildings of his city,
the tiniest bits of the universe that have come to him
and pulled together to be unique in all of time.

This is what he is, and he goes out each morning
to do what the machine asks and comes back each night.
At night the crickets are calling to the darkness and light
within him, and the hum of commerce fills his veins.
He whispers of love with each breath he takes.

This Star-Lit Skeleton of Iron

When my closest friend tells me he is dying, and
that it is important to raise funds to keep the magazine
he edits rolling for as long as his mind stays with him
I am caught in the haze that fills each of us where
words fail because they sound too commercial and
as if they were never made for serious conversation,
and I see instead images that are lights within darkness
as if walking the scaffolding of Brooklyn Bridge without
cars or even girders or support beams or cross wires but
somewhere before the conceptual phase, before it was,
with the stars bright in their constellations above us
and the air around us and the water surging beneath,
the tides as turbulent and bottomless as time itself,
and I tell him after several hours you have borne it well,
the news, the illness, the hours and years you have
dedicated to your first wife and second and children
and most of all to the words of strangers you print
that are swirling all about us because we are brothers
together looking out upon this star-lit skeleton of iron,
this cradle of civilization we have had thrust upon us
and been made aware of without the right tools, and
really they are the right tools, these words we speak
in this time because we are building a bridge, I say.
I don't know where it is going always, but we are.
And the conversation lasts longer than our breath.

The Artist's Home

The artist's home
like the farmer's fields
is filled with the stink of industry.
Turpentine soaked rags stiff
paint brushes scattered on factory floors
left over and turned to upscale condos
without wall room separators just
acres of space between naked window
corridors and an old freight elevator
grain elevator for heavy sides of cow
chicken feathers amber waves of ochre
manure sweat and growing.
What everybody needs to eat
to stay alive grows cheap
and dirty in the elevation of ideals.

The artist's home stinks,
and the art itself carries an aroma
uncomfortable in cocktail circuits.
The musician's screams cornered
in the raw concertina wire of aerials
wound without wings on wolf trap nights,
but like the musk of mink on women,
the fur of Arctic predators against flesh,
a sentient call infuses itself costly
dragging out our bloodlust,
carrying it to coin beneath the stars
and rattling in our boxcars forever
without a name or measure.

What do you see when you walk into a home?
The first home that you're going to buy to live in.
The beds for sleeping…why are they not big enough?
The kitchen for cooking…does it need more than a stove.
A room with table, perhaps a lamp, a sofa, some furniture.

But the house down the street has higher ceilings perhaps,
or more open space filled with what exactly that you pay
   more for
the spaces on the walls that can be filled with what
and of course cathedral ceilings or open stairs
and windows that look out on nature's killing fields.
The space that can be filled with your own nightmares,
or with your inheritors' own undreamed destinies.

Perhaps you put an artist's window on that wall
where you and your guests can sit and peer in
to a cluttered space too large to be contained…
in itself perhaps worth the price of madness
when contrasted with the other window down the hall.
Perhaps it's worth the price of inviting others in
as civilizations before you have done after the trade is in
after the meal is set and fires have burned low
and your woman looks hungry against shadows in the night
like the women of ancient Greece or Rome or Troy
and you come home old and wise with a spear in your hand
and the bill collectors are all lined up by your door
and your faithful hound having slept most of his life
half blind recognizes you and comes to the door
with his heart in doggy recognition thinking god
and dies like that, perhaps in an artist's window on the wall
you have been needing something that comes
in hollow horses that are delivered by enemies in the night.
And perhaps they will set you free on wooden hooves
filled with the dreams of men.

Gathering in The Auditorium

The ticket takers, chair scrapers, janitors,
entrepreneurs, local politicians, national federation members,
drape makers, metal fabricators, microphone holders,
glass blowers and light bulb manufacturers,
cable layers, electricians, coffee baristas, bartenders,
police escorts, paper-pulpers and postal-persons,
limo drivers, parents, children, and children of grandparents
bring their voices together in this room
gathering before the stage and the musicians, speakers,
animators of the mingled voices of our nestling
warming in our very human hearts on a Sunday evening,
taking care of each other, murmuring our affirming diversity
and our contribution to what it means to be among us
in this hall of entertainment built of rock and wood
and shadows, and of the light that draws sound from dark,
erasing boundaries that confirm and disconfirm.

Facets of Jewelry

Cities are condensed studies in contrasts…
the homeless dying by the corner,
the young girl grasping her first diamond…
streetcars of indifference on metal hearts.

Those things that are moved, though,
and are shaped by the human hand
whatever else they are, pick up, are filled,
animated with the fire and spirit of men.

The cities, the jewelry on a night table,
the mechanical contrivances that digitize life.

A Poet's Time And Place

We're spanning ever more time-space
continuum like scientists on this mortal Web
appearing at all hours on any continent,
speaking our words in letters or audio.
Eliot coming in from left field with Prufrock,
Williams with a red wheel barrow in the rain,
Dickey with a sheep child formaldehyde construct
        stored in a bell jar—
the ones who don't answer any more but still talk,
still look out at us and down at their notes,
bringing their *gravitas* into our living rooms
while leaving the smell of old bones behind
in alleyways outside the doors of auditoriums.

We're spanning ever more time-space
continuum each of us as the years go on,
appearing as photons in many places at once
as photons do and in different spheres—
my god, we're almost halfway here for sure,
the language and vision coming at us from
the dead men as well as from your chair
where you are crouched over your groin
touching whatever secrets you find hiding
in the dynamos of human drama, shoulder
ing aside the ghost men and women speaking
as they come and go in a glass jar
enumerating the injustices of daddies and war
tromp tromp but no longer in boot sole rows,
just fading in and out and bright as bugs
before a magic lantern igniting keys,
while fingers fly across a plastic board.

We're appearing in places we have never been
and looking out at things our eyes will never see
in this continuum of ghosts
carrying meaning on blue screens that float away
spanning ever more time-space in our time and place.

The God Particle

Halfway through life
a black hole opened within me
infinitely small sucking
words and images into itself
imploding meaning.
I can send nothing out anymore.

We spend long minutes holding
a live phone line open across the continent.
It is a cell. There are no wires. No landline.
We do not speak but in short bursts
and static silence surrounds us.
Comfort in that, but I wonder at times
between the radio waves whether you are there.
A pillow may be stuffed across your face.
Your hands are turning keys in the silence.
The doorknob rattles and is a cold wind.
Rollover minutes one body to the next.

carioles effect
          trajectory
    velocity
centrifugal mobius space
folded fractals
      cash jingling between stars

Water at sunset
still of wave action
reflects back the heavy stones of time
apartments lived in and left
alleys into shadow
trains into tunnels and clouds
this perfect evening without rain
except that which dries from the air
as the sun goes down goes cool
everything painted in place

by time and reflections.
An eagle poised above time.
What happens when the light goes out
and everything goes on down
into darkness lit up. Undisturbed.

A tow-headed boy in the alley shoots
the big one, the big eagle cats eye shooter
marble from his sweaty fist against the curb
where it shocks back on concrete, reels
and spins its facets among spheres,
particles against particles spinning
in the loose garbage of urbanity
waves ever outward from the hands of a child.
There is something in spinning…
the town the city the universe the cosmos
and the little things as well always the little
giving proof and motion to the large.
Little is a matter of perception and lazy eyes
holding existence in a hand the size of man's brain.

Each pupil is a point in infinity
sucking the light from your world
and imagining you into being

It is the impact that is important
                    spinning in space time
and the splintering velocity
falling deep into the pupils of each eye

on a white shelf in the sunlight
an electric razor lies unplugged
its cord dangling to a marble tile floor
the floor floating on a matted subsurface
unseen but remembered by the pupil
reflecting in a vanity mirror
in a distant room.

Outside The Pinewood Inn

A weathered wooden cross un-engraved
but with bright coins festooned along the cross beam
and a plastic baby's binky tethered by leather chord
lies just outside the provenance of The Pinewood Inn
down beyond the farthest parking lot in Taos.
You won't see it easily, but the workers know,
and a mountain lion that left its print there yesterday
pressed into the dry earth until it takes to wind,
about eight feet beyond the split rail fence, there
behind that first large clump of sage and cactus.

I walked there and saw the lion's paw imprint
and where its nose pressed against the earth, and
I was cold and drew another dime from my pocket,
placing it so that the moon that night would spark
fire from somewhere that thank god was hidden
from me and the pockets of darkness that I know.
I surmise it is a child of the finest spring weather
taken to earth and given passage by its guardians
who live in the mountains rising above our desert.
That there is a child here that they have left
who lies in an opening into the center of the universe,
who like all children in the universe has no name
and carries no gender no baggage no belongings
climbing in and out of the soul we know so little of.

I am caught standing here and thinking these thoughts
as cars pass by in the clean paved parking lot, as wind
scatters the beginnings or ends of years across my feet
while the sun passes lower on the far horizon where
mountain peaks cut short the day and shadows come early.

I am aware of the earth shifting above me and start to rise
with the grains of life still caked beneath my fingernails,
my arms frozen as twisting haloed yuccas, my eyes open
but filled with dirt, not knowing anything I see, not
able to find words to convey what I have already seen.
In the moon you can go so far, you can see across time.

Now in The Confluence of Time

The high plains grasses golden bearded
holding their seeds to dry for spring suns
tossing in a passing wind are in another time
than the mountains rolling above them,
and the fleas leaping from dog to dust
where hunter turns his collar against cold
are in still another time, somehow all caught
in this one meadow outside of Evergreen
where things move slower than they do in Denver
and a woman warms her hands about a cup of tea
watching her reflection in the Starbucks mirrors,
hearing the hum of morning conversations
and the hard slap of coin on counter tops looking
toward the open spaces beckoning beyond paved road
in a time that has nothing to do with digital minute hands.

The Census Taker's Dream

What if each person's DNA is different
    for a reason
not only among the seven billion now alive
washing their skin off in all the rivers of the world,
but among all those who have ever swum the rivers
that have since dried or been dammed
or still carry their immense weight to the depths?
What if there is a collection point matching
the insemination point and the weighing in
not just of words and knowledge and experience
but of each element among all the elements
of the Periodic Table across time laid out
each discovered in its time and enumerated,
each one part per billion, then two, *ad infinitum*
dispersed among one part per billion of each other
being collected, weighed, distilled perhaps
because science only happens when the right parts
come together in the right amounts? The moon
goes red only in a total eclipse; silver drops
from iodide when the mixture is shocked just so.
What if there is a reason for us to know each person
has DNA unlike any other creature in the universe,
unlike any shadow that has passed across constellations,
or that there is no reason that we know but just do,
and that we are all laboratory specimen tubes
rattling among other collection points where
something might happen beyond our knowing?
Knowing each blade of grass has DNA
    unique to its own roots.
There are so many blades of grass
one would think they would come together
or there would be a reason that they would not.

It Is Not The Train

It is the men and women who cry,
the orphans who build boxcars.
It is the prisoners who roll
from cages to build wheels,
the slaves who carry iron
bars across earth for coins
or worse for paper patronage
as dust obscures the rails.

It is not the train that cries,
not the train carrying moonlight
down canyons of no name,
not the train with black boxes
opening to carry seeds of life
to let in the open air of the sea
to fill each box with amber
to move from one lover to another
shaking the earth with its passage
speaking only to the winds.

A Mythology of Our Own

Some say our country has no belief system, no unity.
Yet we do, we have built our own confused mythology
here where men go down to concrete seas in cars,
where we meet in fast food sacristies at edge of time,
where our smelly hides run into each other at each turn
and our music bought from someone else is tuned too loud
yet rumples our hair and jerks our legs as if they were our own.

We know this place we live where no man can hurt us,
where it is the nameless that roll stones to stone us in.
We have the fire in our eye and key chains in our pockets
and a maze of doorways lying open behind us singing
in the winds gathered from urban alleys and aspen mountains
connected by a road of crushed stone and melted tar and time.
How could some say there is nothing left within to open the doors
and creep out wild upon our cities when the sun goes down?

II

Shadows Within The Roaring Fork

The river looks the same as it did
an hour ago, this river that is not a big river
but one you could jump halfway over
one sage brush bank to the other almost,
nothing like the Big Muddy or even The Hudson,
not The Colorado even but still
with the sun hitting down upon its rapids
and spring flush rolling boulders downstream,
with the few shade trees above it in wind
it looks the same river it was yesterday,
a singular presence, an eel chasing its tail
under salt-slicked roadways and arches.

But this is the time of year when most
it changes and the insects hatched upon its surface
are swirled down and kegs of stone roll along
its bed and the minerals giving it its colors
seep into its passage, the fox that dipped its paws,
the bear way upstream that dragged across it
washing the heavy musk of winter in its spume,
have all been taken in its solvent, been drunken deeply
and washed away tasting as nothing but water
in this clearest of mountain rivers erasing it seems
everything and taking it all away within it,
ever changing and taking everything down,
each hoof print, each piece of whitened skull,
each reflection of the moon and the stars,
though it looks the same as it always did.

From far above one day into the next the same,
from up close pressed against your lips, drawn in
from one day into the next it tastes the same purity
of snow that inhabits the highest mountains
having taken all the dust and debris to itself,
roaring that old adage that nothing lasts forever
and even the continents will be washed away.

And perhaps it's so, perhaps the weight
of so many years and souls and dreams
will wash down with the rusted nails
and the broken concrete shells of men,
but entering into that river there are shapes,
are shadows lurking, holding their own
finning the graveling beds, watching,
taking all that debris inside and breathing,
moving independent of the current,
causing change and setting red suns to burn
in places men have not yet gone nor seen.
And these elusive shadows, they change the river as well
filling its waters with the scent and sense of life.

Dr. J.C. McFadden at His Easel in 1919

Another long day today.
Started last night with Miss Cooperman's cough,
then of course Amalio's leg that needed setting,
the Porterman twins coming into the world…
a lot of miles for a worn out horse and buggy,
and a lot of ailments and beginnings for a doctor to attend.

This evening, though, as I sit in my office
watching the sun go down beyond Mount Meeker,
I think of myself as a painter of men, a Van Gogh
with all the colors of Provence right here in Colorado
and a whole universe in my black carry bag.

Look at this briefcase bag of herbal and medicinal tubes
labeled and aligned in rows for portability and mixing.
Feel how I look into a man to find what ails him, and then
I reach among these little tubes and select the pigments
of the earth, the leaves from herbs, the distillate of weeds
and mix them in for him with just the right tint
and I offer it to him as a painter fills his pallet to mend time.

I look at the cavernous rib cage of this skeleton behind me
and know that it contained the love and fire and color,
and the pain as well, and all that goes into a man:
the birds swinging north in springtime, the peeper frogs
filling up the evening with their choruses. These things
a man must have within himself to sing the song of life.
And here I have the tools to listen to his song, the stethoscope
to test the throbbing of his heart, the optical prisms to test
the way he sees the world he brings inside himself,
and then these tubes of earthen pigments again to make him whole.

I can carry so much in the dark bag of delivery I bring:
these are not things you can buy in a store. I am the artist
and the healer and artisan laborer going from door to door.

It Happens Right Here in Loveland, Colorado
at The G&W Sugar Beet Field Processing Plant

There is something sweet and hard in all men
and it is drawn out in our industry from the hard dry ground,
It is drawn out and distilled from our sorrows and our struggles
from working together with our minds and our backs and our
    hands.
It is something at the center of our being, of our reality.

I think of it this time of year, walking knee-deep in the harvest
    fields
as the days grow shorter and the temperature begins to fall. We
    gather,
we neighbors who oversee the farmland, and the migrants, and
    the scientists too,
and the engineers who build factories and railroads and boxcars
    filled with night—
all looking for something sweet and meaningful at the center of
    our being.

We work together as we move through life,
and some of us walk out into the field as I do, and swing knives
    and tools
to shred the dark earth tubers that lie beneath us having drawn life
from the sand and water that lie along the banks of the Big
    Thompson,
within Loveland, we walk the fields rooting out rock hard fruits
    of labor
row upon row of men and women walking the fields in autumn
ripping these beets from the earth, collecting them in piles by the
    roads,
gathering them for processing and refinement, beating down these
    rock hard stones that no man might have thought to eat
but are the transition zone between desert and mountain, arid and
    water,
where we learn to turn our sorrow into the sweet crystals of man's
    soul.

38

We do this every year. We pull the tubers from the soil.

We haul them off the field. We cut off the leaves that bring them sun,

and we shake the earth from them. We haul these gray slabs across the
furrows

of the earth and pile them up for cars built in Detroit and trains built in
Pennsylvania,

and we all work together having come from Russia and England and
New York

and having worked the fields in Mexico and foundries in Chicago,

we come together in this rush of autumn humanity searching for
something

that will enrich and sweeten the heart of our days in Loveland,
Colorado.

We haul these gray tubers away into the dark bins of our days, but we

work with them, we refine them, we cut deeply into what they grew
from,

we lay them out, grate them down, distill their juices. We do this
together:

laborers, scientists, financial wizards who build steel and concrete
monuments,

sweating together to find something clear and sweet within the darkest
earth.

And here we see it, in this vacuum pan chamber where everything
distills like poetry

we see that crystal clear nugget that is at the core of every child's
dream,

something sweet to hang the dreams of a lifetime on where something
sweet

comes from the hardest work that every kind of man and woman can do

working together in the seeding, planting, growing, and harvesting of
seasons.

The Intertype Machine

Hard gray walls of our lives
smooth iron as the factory mills
as the plow blades as the walls of bedrooms
counting out the moments of our early days
in easily handled mouth-size bites.
The news as it shaped our lives the calendars
harvest forecasts sales at the hardware stores
bridal gowns and Mrs. McGinney's bake-sale
weather forecasts ads for seeds to grow
running through the fingers of machines.

You bring them all in here where you can see
and you run them through your hands drop them in
turn them in the guttering candle light. You touch
the letters of each word with only your finger tips,
type them out as slugs upside down and backward.
It takes a careful editor and analyst and printer,
and it takes the right dark ink of time to tell it all
and lay history out the right way round.

This tray here carried all the "I"s,
this one the "o"s, and these the other letters.
Here the En spaces, here the Ems, here the periods
all taken together to keep our daily records,
our planning boards, our letters to the east
attracting the strong young men and women
who would come and build our cities' walls.
Here the essays that led the way to schools.
Here within these all the headlines of our years
the ads for magazine homes and their stories
within while Loveland built its stories
and grew its art.

This machine, this interface with man, sent
our boys off to World War I in 1916, and

it brought some of them back again to sweethearts,
some to enter the ranks of international industry,
and some never to return at all.
It wasn't much...just names on metal and on paper
each a mirror image of each other touched once
    by an old man's finger tips.
Names that lie here now mute, immobile and impervious
still as cast iron stone upon the warm wood boards.

People Wander In And Out of My Understanding

People wander in and out of my understanding
I wear a black armband on the sleeve of my shirt
Things that move my world are unknown to me
Stocks of great companies change hands
while I am playing baseball in center field
Small children are planting rice paddies I am
cold *mano a mano* my arms are cut off twice
before the tiger rises from its lair mouth open

Understanding I wear the sleeve of my shirt
unbuttoned on my armband understandings come
slowly tethered to the eyes of deer in streetlamps
some things come slow in muddy waters
some things peek up between the rushes silent

This goes nowhere you have read reed written
wears woven rafts down muddy waters baby
soft to be discovered on the shore all you need
is to talk across the years and generations that
separate us and the languages long lost to us

We become as one and then disappear into ourselves
without machinery technology exchange commodity
moving ourselves into the awareness of light and
darkness settling into our individual bones and eyes
seeing we become one spider web tangled in the stars
blood passing from husk to husk upon sere wings
seeing everything we do not need to feel I am
what you will become lady and you are open to me

In becoming aware more aware of the torn men/women
through my internet in a far off continent I am aware
less of the papers on my desk and the meat on my table
and your hands settling the covers of my life in New York
or the sworls of your fingerprints across night my DNA

not being the same as yours my knowledge becomes yours
wandering in and out of my understanding where
the eyes of great corporations see not my sleeve
wiped across the sweat of generations.

Driving Alone Across Country

I get into my car just like you.
I am driving across America in the sun rain.
My wife brother drinking buddy sits beside me,
radio CD ripping out Country Chopin Jazz quartet solos
through a wide open closed windshield watching the miles
reflecting stars stoplights moonshine bar signs,
puddling them away into my memory.

This is the way we have always lived,
each one of us in our store bought silk suit jeans
as we hunt for meaning sex loving food meaning hunt
places we have not been yet but remember
in our songs skulls jobs bones weary with work
and walking across an empty parking lot
I get into my car just like you.

Living Alone With You

I spend enough time living alone even with others,
sharpening my teeth on the nail file of time, so why
when amber resins fill the glass in my hands do I
want to gather in the emptiness of your panties
and the hollow howling vacuum of space between
your legs, running up among your spinal column
knuckles kneading themselves against each other,
begging for themselves hands clenched nourishment
from the spaces between constellations oily dark
hidden within their own flesh, distorted, swaying
their song of the equinox muffled from light?

Hold on to me now. Clench tight. I take your
sun bleached hair above fervent closed eyes and
shaking, eager muscles as more than just a sign,
as a divining rod connecting with the mother lode
and the fire that passes between our sun and the grasses
growing wave upon wave across the great plains,
every filament of them absorbing and responding,
glowing in the subtle brilliant colors of Van Gogh
    solar moonscapes

responsive to the wind in ways never imagined,
groaning with an all-consuming hunger. I spend
enough time living alone even with others to know
you will never see this, caught in the immediate,
and will not see the seeds bursting open within you,
and I may forget to mention them myself, but you
bring things different to the world, exotic, erotic
shapes and colors and tongue and scents…hands
that sculpt and fingers carefully enclosing, holding
such things as have never been dreamed before,
and I do my best to understand.

From Kentucky to Tennessee

So much depends
on the eyes in the glass jar
swollen in their formaldehyde
and what preserves them.
This is what keeps us sane.

So Much Silence

The implements of writing litter my life
cigarette butts in ashtrays and whiskey glasses
pens and pencils dried out and broken off
the twisted metal arms of typewriter keys
your words when words were important
and your lips that said what words could not
and computer disks and cloud computing syntax
all the thoughts that Einstein had or Shakespeare
crushed with mine into data bytes, pinheads,
gravel on the shore of the eternal void

but there was so much silence around each space
and so much light glancing off each image
so many inflections in each shift of sound
I could not catch that which was always there.

Invited to Make a Tourist Destination From an
Abandoned Gold Mine, and Call it Art
in Hinsdale County, Colorado

What can you make of rock tunnels chiseled
open between the fingers of dead men's hands,
beneath twisted pine trunks and endless winters
that will draw tourists to this mountain town?
What kind of doodlebugs will you light
from the tallow of forgotten miners' minds
now that the single lines of rusted track leading back
into your intestines have been removed and sold
and you are filled with the icy cold of time
warming your hands around the jewels it holds?
What will you do to replace this gold now gone
to tell its story in the containment vaults of Fort Knox?
Surely, whatever it is you make will be of art,
for it will come from the vacant spaces man has shaped.
And it will come in lunch boxes at the end of day.

I suggest that windows be placed within the slagheap,
lighting the stifling spaces where men worked collapsed
imprinting them into fossil images of humanists, and that
the music fed into your museum be of the wind barreling
through the twisted roots of stars across an open universe.
I suggest that you remove the stench of men's sweat and
wash down the dried urine around each blind corner, clap
castanets on your fingers, bring in the cotton candy, build
a merry-go-round at its slumping entrance and hang a pail,
a dented tin pail beside a sign in bright red paint saying
Here's where to put your tips in now you've seen the gold,
and run a four lane highway up there with gambling casinos
and put lots of bright-lit mirrors on the empty walls
and see if that won't bring them in, keep them off the street.

Seen Once in 60 Years

We were on the mountain
the day the aspens opened.
Each of them acre upon acre.
Paper trunks of yesterday fringed,
opened and began to green
obscuring granite and mica,
unfolding the legs and wings,
fleshing out the skeletons,
in only one evening we were
transformed beyond understanding.

We were beyond green
and were the color of old stone
when it came upon us and grew
within behind our hoary bony faces
etched from ashes we had sewn.
Nothing holds and nothing held
but framework breathing sun.
It is just these littlest things now
that carry light across the universe
and make life of it. You know.

After a Summer Hail Storm

Red tail hawk descends the Front Range
foothills, chills talons twenty degrees.

At seventy years log walls under pressure
crack settling into the spaces left behind.
Form follows function once again
What do steel beams do? Gold bullion bars,
   given time?

Aspens stripped of their leaves by hail
sprout spring fresh baby green leaves
too late less than two weeks hence if
there is time before winter sets in again.
Both ice and life feed on the sun and
their roots are buried deep in bedrock.

Sound of a Nighthawk

I lay awake for a long while
after the harvest was gathered in
and the fancy stemmed glassware
had been drained of its wine,
and I listened to the earth.
A coyote beyond the golf course
filled its throat with the moon.
Its sound did not match the clock
ticking on the wall of my study.
A syncopation and a ululation
left something dancing between.
Claws swept across my back.
Then the sound of a nighthawk.
Something I have never seen
that carries dusk upon its feathers,
eating little things that fly away.

The Body Beating on Its Own Heart

Standing in this alpine meadow among fallen chimneys
and dirt streets paved over with years of weeds, where
snow blew three outbreaks of cholera across the west,
I remind you of the recent picket fences now gone that
lay along the edge of Caribou cemetery and the stones
scattered with scraps of letters carved into eternity,
snapped off sudden in the cold or in some tourist's hand.
Now, with the jeep roads opened up and traveling what
it has become, though there only a handful of years ago,
the cemetery is gone and graves lie beneath trails
where only human soles and the pads of animals and
more cold beyond cold moves over them in night.

But the dry grasses that fill this alpine meadow start to
turn in the early autumn air, flaring paint brush heads
red amber gray and sunrise yellow across the hills, and
our breath takes flight on the cry of red tailed hawks
circling a point that has no point in place or time. A
beating as of drums starts up within receding canyons,
echoing distantly in the frost-heaved stones, then closer,
begins to echo, throb, within my own bones and my heart
too takes up the funereal song of everlasting life,
the body beating on its own heart.

What We Are Going Through in This Time

Whatever disturbs your pure flesh
        that grew from the pine forests and alpine lakes
    whatever disturbs your mind as it cares for the animals
as it strikes the chords of the eternal cosmos
        it is true is but a moment in passing life
but it wounds you and distorts you from the winds
that carry across our place in time and history
and because it disturbs your flesh it does your mind
as it does all of our minds in this awful time
        as our minds are born of flesh and spirit

we must rise beyond the flesh that weakens us
and beyond the mind that can be caged by fear or hate,
and we must understand in our flesh the power of words
and the arrows and hatred and fear they can bring
        and Death, that too,
and how to use them ourselves as shamans once did
or as phoenixes that flew above the fires of Homer
and rose from the ashes more powerful more horrible
        than what had sought their death

and so this is what I say to you, what I leave you
across every breakfast table in America every home
where a husband and wife are looking across time
and each of them are looking the same way each
    of them are looking across every breakfast table
as the sun is rising over the tired buildings they inhabit
the commercials playing on their radio and TVs
and the pages of the small town newspapers they turn
as they wait for the coffee to cool just a little more
are all saying the same thing but are still missing
what each one of them might say before the day begins
and must say before the sun goes down on our time,
and if they do then each one of them will change the world
and oh your pure flesh though scarred will be of all that is holy.

What Men Will Die For

Words read from books
by their mothers
who look beyond office windows
when the body gives out
at the end day.

The sergeant
giving orders on the wings
of death at dawn

A woman who smells
of Saks Fifth Avenue and
something that is of herself

Children who are open hearts
beating in the light beneath stars
that he carries within his chest

Alphanumeric equations
played across violin strings
in songs by Einstein and Oppenheimer
pressed into digital equations by Google Earth

The little things that mean everything
where words first open on an intake of breath
and then let their meaning out into the night

A punch card, a time clock, and all that is noble.

Coming Home From The War

What happens in a man's circle
is what matters in his time.
The fish rise in evening.
The smells of summer are his.
The girls down by the river
bathe in lilac and vanilla.
When his circle holds
the crickets in the meadow
maintain space with the frogs
    in the pond.
The fish are all silvery trout
with the moon on their scales.
The investment banker cannot
    intervene,
is but a cicada in her long
    slow cycle of sleep and frenzy
down among the roots of dreams.
All rooms in the cabin are his
and newscasters bide their time
    toward wisdom in silence
in his time.

October Afternoon by a Log Fire

I see what has not changed
for generations weathered plank boards
beetle holed and solid as flies' eyes
within electric lights and heat
in generations gone

        Hitler, Stalin, Trotsky, Stalin
    Churchill, Mussolini, Hirohito, FDR, Initials
          these walls built in a homecoming
      a returning soon becoming a retreat.

Mountain pines and aspen change. Asters
  wilt. Bears have returned and cougar
  Moose too   one wolf half starved a year ago
    in the foothills.
Lodge pole pine and ponderosa
grown from scrub willow groves
Now gone and the aspen yet again
   leaves luminous in dusk
Trout gone into forever pools and riffles
          metaphoric stars
The stars though still the same
high distance on a cold autumn night

        Each season has excuses.

Windy cabin on the hill we keep pictures on the walls
    Uniforms
   Old tea pots, doilies, table cloths, a scrubbing board.
The cold passes through
We stuff the chinks with mortar
  quick-set by mountain streams
and fire the pot belly stove inside
with the boughs of trees and even seeds
in the distance of our birth

Old dust in cupboards
Marshall music on a distant breeze
Wagner across candlelight
as the constellations wither.

Learning to Drive

Before I died I propped myself up and watched
the Leonid meteor shower over New York City,
each molten stone etched across one vast glass,
for 20 minutes a torrent of heat and light across
horizons cutting through chimneys and furnaces.
You were scared and attentive and held my hand
but when they released me three weeks later you
said there were low clouds that night and no light
as far as you or others in the city could see. And

so I've thought about that ever since, and the cold
between the clouds between stars between time,
and I've thought of how we sit before computers
and how we sit before television sets and bar signs
and how they reflect from puddles in dark alleys,
their red eyes bleeding deep into our cold wet bones.
I've watched insects dance frenetic beneath lamps
with a subtler sense of the futilities perhaps but
knowing nothing gained is nothing lost and then

there was something passing quickly above us,
something as hard as the atoms of which we're made
and as fast as the thoughts inside our tired minds,
and we would have seen it if we had not made what
we made that we could give a name. And passing
in itself brings light and friction and heat and seeds
germinating, and what goes out comes back across.

The radio in my car is often on but is turned off on
nights we are alone. The cell phone in my pocket
is muted and dead metal. The pager thrown away.
We are learning to drive across the desert. The city
that we left behind us is nothing more than sand.

The Hudson Line

Getting on the commuter train I track more snow
and foot crud from fellow passengers than God
into the aisles between the scrubbed down seats,
and looking down I wonder where it all comes from
dappling in those disgusting dents of linoleum tile.
I mean, the snow falling from the sky is white
and the air so clear it seems to disappear in time
but the black gunk keeps on rising from the ground
everywhere a tired man has put down his boot sole
or a young girl has danced across a dancehall singing
of things that don't have anything to do with what is dark,
and I don't know how it has all congealed upon my feet.

By the time the train has gotten me home, I have left
all the broken curses and shattered paychecks where they fell,
hardly thinking of the gray man who will mop up after me
and of how he will smell of what I leave behind when he leaves,
but I gather up the part of me I left in suburbia in the morning
and I leave the city behind me when I leave the car tracking
north toward Sleepy Hollow where the snow is still deep
up through the beginnings of the old Rockefeller estate
the disposable skin of which has been sold now to the state
where the path I walk winds among forgotten grave stones.

Each step heavier than the last, harder to lift through crusted cold
and my leather office shoes soaking water in like wet cardboard,
mind too melting slowly away into the cold of time I climb
away from the river and the old mill where revolutionaries ground corn
and I keep walking away from my home into the night where I see
horsemen passing across my path without leaving any prints at all,
and I think of my wife and children growing distant in their warmth
by the oven in the kitchen with its meal warm as my heart once was,
and I wonder what it will mean after all of this to go home
again and go out again to my office and my papers
when the train meshes its awful wheels again and breathes slow.

In the morning, though, one doesn't think of this, and dreams
of what one did today or yesterday are drawn thin as billfolds,
the train itself going both ways indifferent into dawn and night
and no knowing if it's your flesh or mine pressed upon its skin.

Don't Walk

There is a time each day
that Edgmont Street stretches empty
past pastel empty houses toward
Long's Peak on one end and
the upper Platte Water Shed
through concrete tunnels on the other
near where empty warehouses house
the machinery that gives us love
that no woman's eyes touch
first chill grayness of day nor
ears hear the splash of empty pave-
ment traveling forever into time,
that ghosts do hold this town their own
and pause before the Do Not Walk
signs silently gathering just a moment
in breeze dropped shadows the way
you might see them from the corner
of your own eye waiting on the corner,
only the lack of motion giving them away
waiting to be told by the light of day
don't walk walk don't walk again
and again until the sun rises up again
and our souls are hard as tanned leather
or the eyes of spring heifers climbing
to their legs in the high country coming home.

With No Tomorrow

I have been finding a place of ecstasy
that lies outside letters and words,
that is buried in Paleolithic drawings
chipped away by several thousand years
and is still untranslated by universities…
the red ochre on sandstone from what is
carpeted in the space of stars in time, a man
of stick figure intent against unspoken word.

And I am here now, whispering in your ear
my gratitude at having found you sleeping
defenseless to my entry. We will rise stronger.
Throw out your twitter keypad and diaries.
They will not staunch the blood of our wounds.
I am in you growing into a gender you do not
understand this is not politically correct in any
way down upon the swanky rivers far far away,
that's where my harp is calling me ever far.
Angel I have loved you since the day before you
were dreamed and will find you after my death.

The wind outside my desert porch balcony
beneath the Big Dipper and Cassiopeia gusts
atoms into the vast space of time and swirls
nothing against my flesh that I will remember
and I revel that in this instant of impossibility
the scent of your flesh fills my nostrils and
your eyes are what my mind remembers at night,
my darling when accountants fall asleep and all
is a final smoothing into ecstasy with no tomorrow.

III

Love in Quantum Field Theory

I am awake with the mountain cats,
perturbations in the shadows of nothingness.
There are four fields in quantum theory,
open flowings without fences,
dimpled with the circles of disruption
splashed from infinite possibilities on themselves,
of those things that go through a cat's eye
and are the eye of the dark cat beyond night,
night-light within the beginning of all things.

We circle around upon through each other, bosons,
each dimpled ripple seeking something in the curve
that entwined without mind in the dimpled curve
is sensed most perfectly as being what we need
as things that have no needs beyond ourselves.

And I don't know now as dusk settles time space
like a liquid crystal cat display in window glass
what gravity this has that causes the fields
to feed upon themselves, to flow between
the stones that are the field or the flesh.
Perhaps a field out beyond the fences built
will be found to flow between the currents
ebbing forever in the tidal flow. Perhaps

there is nothing that can disrupt field theory
dimpling on itself except some other force
where life finds life within each other
creating not another like itself but life
creating what no other force can feel or be,
switching back and forth a lover's lazy gaze
sinuous as the dreams of anything, falling
through everything with the weight of life
lost in the majesty of mindless certainty.
Appearing.

While I Am Aware

Whatever moves above the light
moves below the light.
There are shadows.

As long as my flesh
hangs onto my bones,
I will long for your touch.
I understand this does not
make me attractive to you.

When you are gone
these things will not matter.

Why The Man Wore Red Shirts

Fred carried a weasel under his jacket.
His friends thought its heavy breathing was his heart.
but at meetings it would gnaw on him,
and in bed it would hang from his left nipple.

Taking Out The Green Green Grass to Grow

It takes a long time to take out
the grass that grows outside suburban homes
in order to plant my own vegetables.
It takes my father's old, worn shovel
driven down through gray mats of roots,
hour beyond hour for two days to dig
like a farmer cutting through the grass
of gardens and the sod of civilization
rather than raising wheat where he should,
ripping out old chunks of forgotten fences
with the blade and neglecting urban duties
for just one small bed of garden of my own,
then shifting out the rocks by hand and
rattling the dry clods of clay from roots
to smooth the soil for spreading mulch
composed of last year's leaves and clippings
stored in a corner outside last year's harvests
by the back door where the dog comes in.
And it takes a long time to build the frames
that even I know are needed to keep separate
what I grow from what I own at home.
But eventually, these will be things I eat
that I have grown, and it takes so long to grow
and longer still to lay the ground around you
in a land where all that comes about comes
increasingly in paper bags and plastic
and never feels the rains or cold of night.

Barbed Wire Marking The Perimeters

It takes longer than a lifetime for barbed wire to rust away,
longer than the hands of the man who ran it up will last.
A hundred twenty years for many of these Colorado homes
and the cut dust banks that used to line their wagon roads.
The elk and bear and moose still live here in these alpine glens.
You can track them easily after rain, though few today still do,
and you can find strands of their hair and even skin caught
on those sharp barbs where they lie twined in loose loops
buried under the white dried grasses, the Oregon grapes, quartz
veins that lead an argument of insidious intent into the gold
dreamed of and fought for by older generations than ours, still
holding onto something brown that rubs off on your hands.

Do We Not?

We get older do we not?
The brick walls around our lives
are felt more carefully, lovingly,
the moss grown into their mortar
greener and more a thing to love.
The coins rattling in casino halls
a shrilling muttering of our bones,
masks of comedy and tragedy
both gaping open mouthed stares.

We get older do we not?
The voices that once touched all
as they grow quieter raise volumes.
Walking in the woods scattering
last autumn's sun gatherers
as the first green fern fiddlers rise
from darkness and earthy mold
the voices that once touched all
enlighten our own songs with silence.

We do get older do we not
or is it just the flesh sagging down
to rest as we grow closer among
the *mardi gras* celebrations of bone
the wickered baskets of old women
the stone corridors of Spanish forts
the musings of *australia pithecus*
reaching toward an unlit tunnel
with opposable thumbs and tongue
scattering the wind where it will.

Something I've Wanted to Tell You Of

There is a tunnel under the house
up against the bluff by the willow,
the old one built of dark red stone
which has stood vacant for ten years.
It lost its lower windows last winter
one afternoon while I walked alone and
threw small stones against the wind.
I could hear them shatter across time,
each window separating in the now,
and so crawled in just to see what was
there under the threadbare carpet
at the back by the pantry, a casual
glance to make sure all was well still,
when I found that heavy trap door
and scarred wood steps leading down
to where mirrors lined earthen walls
leading off into our mountainside.
Not wide, maybe five feet of aisle
open between the lights and chairs,
everything covered with a fine dust
so you could still see the marks
where something heavy was dragged
deeper in or father out often enough
the men who lived there moved away.

Sometimes the ground shakes late
at night when trucks haul the moon away
down their driveway and past our gate.
Over the ice in my whiskey glass
I can hear the laughter of those men
entwined with the roar of their engines
which alone are enough to shake our home.
But not once have I gotten up to look,
not once because they only come at night
and the house is vacant, as I said,
and there are no tire tracks on the road

in the morning, no dust blowing in the wind,
and I've reflected too long on what I saw
at the farthest end where the light ran out.
It's something I've wanted to tell you of.

In Another Passage

It is after I return home exhausted,
and I lean forward and my fingers run
back and forth across my knees.
It has been a difficult day and my hands
feel for human touch in the threads woven
by machines in far eastern countries.
I think of summer time and the livin' is easy
and know these machines are the same as American
machines in the industry we have lost to musicals.

I lean forward and my fingers interrupt your
wanting to lie back upon the sofa and watch TV
while the Trojans emasculate our country on Saturday Night Football.
I am snoring too, I have to admit, though I love you.

I remember one summer day when it was ninety in the shade
we took off, stole an hour together and climbed into a canoe on the
    reservoir
that watered all of New York City and we poled out into the water
and the pole stuck deep into the mud as I swept us outward so that
I had to throw myself into the water, escape the mud, and swim,
pulling us back into a shaded overhead where we took off our clothes
and laid them out to dry in the wind while we naked were too cold
to do anything but watch the water move inward toward the land.

I study the creases in these fingers I run across my knees,
and remember cupping your buttocks after we had all but dried,
and brought forth the springs of youth again that day,
and how the cars of a multitude flew by twenty feet away that day
on the highway of America that would take us each away.
It has been many years and it may be that you are gone.
My fingers meet with those that filled the loom
selling for thirty bucks in any downtown store.

I live in Colorado now, up against the mountains,
climbing trails far from where the urban masses dwell

and what I touch with my fingers is mostly memory
with one single element that distills it all and
the scent of your flesh upon these fingers after all
these years not quite mechanized upon the loom.

The Way Things Are

A friend of sorts comments by email
that America has never had mountain poets
who retire from the military or corporations
to wander across the miles of our culture
weaving their thoughts from dry grasses
or filling their songs with mountain storms.
Maybe the closest we come to such intellects,
he says, may be hidden in Vietnam vets
dropping off the map for the Adirondacks.
I know there are a few living there, have heard
that they generate their own wind power
while crafting covers for the words of others
and pinch their offerings into the national flotsam.
I nod, though, because I know of none who was
a general who led armies before retiring there
to write like Li Po with his dragons.

We do not mix killing with our little sonnets—
not the kind we teach in classrooms. Nor do we
mix the passions we feel for men and women
whom we encounter at the drugstore or supermarket
with the things mountain men dream of or observe.
And the resources of wolves and caribou and moose
are limited in the way they can disperse words within
our multicultural monoclonal international media.
Whatever the beauty of a grain of alpine grass
poking its way through the dried grey white of
cabin boards that have fallen away to earth, it does
not leave the harsh loud mark of ink on money.
You're right, I say, the life we move among once
having left the cities and Washington behind us
is too subtle to be heard above the roars of cars
rushing America to the faceless offices we knew.
It will last too long for us to talk about, and so
we hold our peace within ourselves. We speak
amongst ourselves, but we do no not travel well.
It is too bad, but that's the way things are.

Where the Web Is And Where It Is Not

Write about Nederland and Eldora, the tourist shops,
schools, mountain towns, nurseries for the troops deploying
to protect their homeland from the tourist shops of the Mid-East.
The log cabins, tin trailers, recreational weed shops of Colorado
where the boys want to fly on metal wings. This day it was
a day of sudden squalls and flash floods in the high mountains
across the Continental Divide, and of monsoon rains
from the Front Range to India and Pakistan and Syria, a day
when Eldora and Ward, Colorado, with their insignificant
   population
were off the Web and dark rooms at sea were filled
with magnetic pings and electronic order for the mountain boys.

A Poem to be Finished Later

Don't die in the little rooms with white sheets.
Don't die where it is easy and there is no pain,
where no owls twist their talons beneath the moon,
where shadow takes you suddenly oh no.

Go not into the intravenous drug cave.
There is only one pain in all eternity to know.
Go not back from the battle when all is lost,
but let the shadow find itself going out
and leave a word your being can hold oh.

Acting on Actionable Intelligence

All the sifting is done here
in this soundless room with soft speaking men.
The culmination of analysts and spreadsheets
pixels gained from satellites
phone calls from loose lips
drug busts outside opium dens
desert sand boxes the turning of heavy turrets
the sums of dead bodies and workers
driving out the GNP and world economy
into digits that can be expressed in the hum
lost in the acrid stench of sweat and fear
coiled in massive electronic mountains
around the core of this womb. Here
is where we become a part of the machine
and fire flows from our collective fingers
pouring cruise missiles, bunker busting bombs,
or boots on the ground containing
all we have imagined and been told,
spitting it out across the globe to erase
whatever cells start to grow outside the mold
The machine speaks through my fingers.

I am a part of the rows of dead children
who would have carried bombs in their bellies
to blow apart the institutions I have built
on the money that melts down metal for tanks
and jewelry, for birthday presents and trinkets
in the roar of a world composed of data and fact
crushing against Gilgamesh and war and poetry
where each child is a universe eternal to itself
before the herding and the sifting has begun.

I am sitting here like Randal Jarrell within
the death of the ball turret gunner pressing
my fingers on buttons but at a distance now
inside a womb where nothing can get out or in
except the electricity that fires our minds
and our machines on their integrated wires
and circuitry that is constantly refined by data
dumps and indiscretions and fights in Washington,
sitting here and pressing buttons as if it is the end,
so far from where blood explodes it makes no matter.
We'll have a meeting with the monsters in an hour.

I know at the end of the day a man cannot keep his mind
in such a hub of media persuasion and electronic noise
in a room of buttons that anyone can press if kept calm,
where individuals mean little more than bodies in the sand.

Above The Fence That Now Lies Rusted

Mr. Kendridge strung up a barbed wire fence
low to the ground back in 1939. A hard year
didn't want some other man living higher up
the mountain. Still just wagon ruts running up,
but he's gone three generations now and we're
still growing columbine and tufted mountain
squirrels and elk above where he grew his anger.
Lots of thoughts come off that hillside and grow
both ways across the continent, wafting through
the night tight lattice of a country's thought.
Jim went into law, Joe design, Fos architecture,
and Sue married two men at least and left
children in Hollywood and Washington and
books like this one written here with a spine
bent backward with the weight of business and
politics and urban planning and feeding families
never thought of before a man opened up that mine,
took fire-hardened trees with the resin baked in
to hold back the rigors of aging and fire and built
a cabin way up above that fence that now lies rusted
still snaking broken over the weed-choked ground.

At Night in a Timeless House

Sometimes a man builds a house
around a particular spot of land
where a story is waiting to be told,
or buys one at the spur of the moment.
And sometimes he is the one to tell
what darkness or fire burns there,
and sometimes it is another. It is
his wife after he has left the room,
or his next door neighbor visiting
then carrying something away in mind,
or it is a grandchild moving in after
the old hinges spring from the doorway
and have been replaced again and again.

This is one of those houses you are in,
looking almost the way you wanted
but with clocks that tick too loudly,
computer screens that suddenly glow
blue in the night of refreshing memories
or downloading extra security updates,
drafts that chill the floor in winter,
open spaces out beyond the shadows
of your bookcases and spreadsheets,
the scuttling of toe nails up the walls,
the consciousness of something living,
an awareness watching from the basement
filling its dark eyes with wondering
and finding peace in what passes, food
in the night corridors when you sleep
at the beginning of our understanding.

Perpetually Crossing The River

I get up in the middle of the night and pour a chardonnay.
It is light and in the darkness reminds me of your lips.
You are sleeping somewhere I am not allowed to be,
but all things not allowed are what I carry through life.
We have chosen the moonbeams that will imprison us.
I like drinking after everyone in the family goes to sleep.
Then in the day, I go out and look up strangers' phone numbers
and addresses. I slip unwritten checks beneath their doors.
Someday, I think, I will write you a letter about them all.
The moon rises inside a cup of hand-crafted sands, and Charon
rows back and forth across it with his dog in his lap snuffling
at everything that comes before him and all that has been.

Brighter Than These Things That Last

I think of your young limbs
rising from fields of prairie grass,
how you flex on the balls of your feet
while their grains rise up along your thighs,
how impatiently they thrust against you and
how impatiently you tune your laughter
to the sunlight that fills each grain
and the moon that bathes each stalk.

So much is scattered between words
cigarettes drawn into the lungs scattered
bricks upon concrete alleys books gum
wrappers zip-locked sandwiches and
inked up time clocks in the rain squalid
with the scent of unwashed wishes and cityscapes.

Each of these and infinitely more as seeds
blowing across this sun soaked meadow,
each seed absorbing all it needs to send
seeds into the vacuum tube of time and you
sprinting from seed to seed to gather them,
melting them down into your flesh hot sun
you burn brighter than these things that last.

Even When It Is Coldest

Winter on the mountain.
A spark rises from the fireplace
as we sit waiting into the night.
We sit night after night no phone
because no factories above us,
no ski lifts this side of the peak
no houses that are occupied,
just the frozen wetlands
the snow weighted pine shrubs
where moose look out at dark
and see whatever moose see
from the millennia of their lives

but it's just this winding down
each evening after rush of day
and cutting logs chopping ice
for the horses so they can drink
from the waters that ran last fall,
this stagnation at the center of
call it industry or eternity or feeling
when the candles are too low
and the light to read by too dim
and conversation turns to boards
nailed together forty years ago,
that spark rising is a big thing,
and it might implode the night.

Such times we talk of liquid eyes
looking out from river otters
and of our own young ones
what they will do when June opens the roads
and how far they will go then,
knowing it is cold and we burn
all that we can gather in a short time.

And words fail us at last, like light
which burns down in the cabin yet
lights up constellations we can't see,
and we turn to each other in bed
our fingers feeling what our futures hold
and embracing children drawn of the gods
from within the memories of spring we hold
no words that are really the stuff of flesh and life
going in and out beyond time and light.

Across Star Time

We are the last people on Spencer Mountain
in the last house built above Marysville in 1940
where dirt roads still wind among abandoned mines,
last fall's flood and this spring's hundred year melt
having washed walls and hand hewed bridges away.
It is cold for early June and the fire burning high
in our log cabin beneath the high full moon.

In this silence the transference of life across
the cosmos is evident in the aspen log burning
in our forgotten space far from the universities
where I have taught words, memories of scholars.
This tree that grew in darkness tethered to others
as only aspen trees grow, hearts hidden in soil
where the world appears to give out no light
growing on the ephemeral spirit of the sun alone
boughs stretched out forty years, took life from light
before its outstretched limbs dried and broke. This
dead log now giving heat to a man who would write
books lit by something substantial across star time.

Being With You at Timberline

The longer we spend in this log cabin
without news feeds nor talking heads watching
aspen and pine burning down to red as eyelid ashes
the more we start to know each other after
thirty years, and the more the rest recedes,
the less we know of ephemera or of the men
who dodge between countries keeping us safe:
men I used to work among and thought important.
Names on neckties now in jobs gone bad, or
holding hands with butchers beneath the field.
I like to think that someone still fills the bill,
but it isn't me. I cut some wood this afternoon,
caught a mess of trout down by Barker Reservoir,
came home, and in coming home,
lit the fire again.

Finding Tunnels Above The Mountain

It isn't metaphor. Every autumn when the mountain dries
and the leaves lying close to the ground turn red in evening,
long tunnels of baked adobe appear, crossing the ruts of road
we walk along, running off into the meadow, down to the highway,
off into the landslide skree and jumbled mine dumps. Suddenly
there and perfect in their wanderings when we rise in morning.
They're probably caused by moles or something like them,
small dark animals inside the darkness of their own warmth
working and digging with the enthusiasm of their own love
and pushing their soft faces into the harsh, dry earth with joy,
I think, and see in my mind their outsized swollen pink hands
waving before their faces which are absolutely blind in
their softness and eagerness to get somewhere. They think,
perhaps, of roots, of giant turnips that do not grow here,
and their fleshy appendages push everything away before them.

Not Much Has Changed

Not much has changed in this death.
A child who would have been as good a friend
perhaps or had as much compassion and passion
and love of life perhaps lives somewhere,
and it does not matter that I will never know him.

I will remember the coffees at old wood tables,
the strumming of guitar, the way notes melted into pain,
the charities we organized together for the working man
knowing that we had worked the hot steel ovens of the 60s
and each alone had headed out across the desert of America
and each alone had found our love and wives and peace
sooner than we should but too far from where we started.

These are personal things that do not mean a damn
to those things that we both believed in. The sun rising
beyond the mountains on an autumn morning. The aspen
going gold into the slow detritus of the coming winter
and the wind whipping mountain peaks even as today.
A colder time is coming warmed only by memory.
Not much has changed, and he would say the same.

Scattered Memories of Those Forgotten

Maybe it would have been different if the graves
weren't enclosed in a wrought iron fence still polished
like the day they were laid out a century ago, names
from ages past but looking carved just yesterday,
or if we hadn't driven miles down a dirt road to be here
with no sign of people and the road but eight feet wide
and willows and branches up against the doors scratching
and it was getting on toward evening beneath low clouds,
or if there was any sign of the town it came from once
or if the people buried there lived out their lives
without the government coming in three times and
taking everything away from them and closing factories,
and heck, this was just one of 200 to 300 graveyards
counted by the government along this strip of land,
 but they're not quite sure of names, numbers, or families,
and boarding up the iron mines those men operated
and telling the survivors the sons and daughters to move on,
grab whatever scraps of money they were offered
without bargaining or trials or anything back in 1933,
just take what yer offered and consider yourself lucky
and maybe over the years come back and see the graves
after the TVA has moved on. But I don't know, it's
posted as a National Recreation Area now, this land
between the lakes where these dead lie buried,
and what's that say?

Maybe it was the stillness that lay over the land
or something pulling me in, drawing me thin,
as I stood there looking, but graves do strange things
to the living in all kinds of ways, and I just stood there
a few moments and saw maybe 80 graves of women
by their names at least and miners and ore processers
and the keepers of what stood for sanity in the Depression,
and I remembered the worn faces and the molten iron
the heavy axes weathered by the hands of men in photos

back at the little modern building at the entrance to the
land between the lakes between yesterday and tomorrow
between two Appalachian rivers dammed by the TVA
for what's been named a National Recreation Area
as it turned the lights on in America, and I wondered
what kind of light what kind of power can come of that
that you would want to light your way into the future.

And maybe it was that kind of thought made me nervous
or the mists floating over the graves made me nervous
and made me think of men looking down their gun sites
coming up behind me, but the other thing I saw there
scattered among those ornate and simple tombstones were
small white crosses you might make out of pop sickle sticks
 just standing there scattered all around as well maybe a hundred
all around scattered without a pattern over stones beside mounds
on top of them and over there by the far corners as well, and I
didn't feel right about going in to see what they were about,
and so I didn't get too close and got back in the car and drove
until I left that blasted ground and its lost lives and dreams,
and maybe those white crosses marked small bits of bone
found by archeologists and who knows what those bones were
or maybe they were tourists who got too curious or were dreams
or more terribly yet the scattered memories of those forgotten
scattered from the town folk themselves rising to fruition.
I'm only telling you because its off a side road, way back,
and the chances are you won't come across it anytime soon at all.
It don't mean much anyway, just another shadow in the night we know.

Only The Commentator

The technology is in your mind
separate from your buttocks swelling
the warmth of you abdomen
the enclosure of your womb.
It is beyond your eyes and senses
somewhere in the music of darkness

where there is no machinery no
steel or plastic containment, no
separation from the cells of your dreams
because technology breaks it all down
and what you envision you become
and what you think you can do
has somehow been done by others
and by you in the instant of need.

You are in the century beyond tomorrow
within the life realm that has always been,
and science is a glimmer on the past horizon.

Acknowledgments

Poems in this book first appeared in the following publications, to whose editors I wish to express my thanks:

After Hours for publication of "Above The Fence That Now Lies Rusted"

Big City Lit for "A Poem to be Finished Later," "Driving Across Country," "Learning to Drive," "People Wander In And Out of my Understanding," "Seen Once in 60 Years," and "Where The Web is And Where it is Not"

Casa de Cinco Hermanas for "Don't Walk," "Now in the Confluence of Time," and "Outside The Pinewood Inn"

Chiron Review for "Brighter Than These Things That Last," "Even When it is Coldest," "Shadows Within The Roaring Fork," "Something I've Wanted to Tell You Of," and "This Star-Lit Skeleton of Iron"

Heavy Bear for "Barbed Wire Marking the Perimeters" and "With No Tomorrow"

Ibbetson Street Review for "A Poet's Place And Time" and "It Is Not The Train"

Liquid Light Press for "How Do You Look At This Space?"

Louisiana Literature for "He Does What It Takes"

Loveland Museum & Gallery's Permanent Collection for "Dr. J.C. McFadden at His Easel in 1919," "It Happens Right Here in Loveland, Colorado at The G.W. Sugar Beet Field Processing Plant," and "The Intertype Machine"

Lyrical Somerville for "What Men Will Die For"

Mind Magazine for "Love in Quantum Field Theory"

Mountain Gazette for "Why the Man Wore Red Shirts"

Pilgrimage Magazine for "Across Star Time"

Poetry Bay for "Deep in The Convenience Store"

Presa for "Do We Not"

The Same for "Sound of a Nighthawk" and "Leaving The Hudson Line"

Turtle Island Quarterly for "A Mythology of Our Own," "The City Within The City," and "How Do You Look At This Space?"

Wilderness House Review for "The God Particle" and "October Afternoon by a Log Fire"

About the Author

Jared Smith is the author of thirteen volumes of poetry, two CDs, and multi-media stage presentations in New York and Chicago. His poems, essays, and literary commentary have appeared in hundreds of magazines and anthologies in this country, Canada, Mexico, the U.K., China, and Hong Kong over the past half century. He is Poetry Editor of *Turtle Island Quarterly*, and has served on the Editorial Boards of leading literary magazines, including *The New York Quarterly*, *Home Planet News*, and *The Pedestal Magazine*. He has also served on the Board of Directors of literary and arts non-profits in New York, Illinois, and Colorado. He is a former Director of Education and Research for an international research institute, as well as former advisor to several White House Commissions under President Bill Clinton, and Special Appointee to Argonne National Laboratory. He has served on the faculty of New York University, LaGuardia Community College, and Illinois Institute of Technology. Jared currently lives outside Boulder, Colorado and spends much of his time at an unimproved log cabin deep in Roosevelt National Forest where the nearest neighbors are bears, elk, and moose.